My Daughters Are Having Boy Problems

Marzell Mitchell

Copyright © 2020 Marzell Mitchell

All rights reserved.

ISBN: 9780578779058

Dedication

To my daughters, Shaneick, Natiiya, Quatisha, Jaya, Breshanna, Nykkia, KeKe, Kiyha, Tikerra, Zyri, and Mayja. It is truly a blessing from God that we are meant to be family. God could not have chosen better molds from which to create my golden girls. Thank you for sharing both your experiences and questions about what makes boys think, do, and who they are. I hope and pray that I have shared enough information to help you learn and grow in your relationships, maybe even in ways you hadn't thought about.

To the friends I connected with at Maxwell F.P.C in the years 2008-2010. You made my stay well rounded and encouraged my mind. Your life journeys have been an inspiration to my growth and achievement of success. The place of worship encouraged my soul. A heartfelt thank you to Chaplain and First Lady Fisher. I'm forever grateful.

To Netta, thank you for helping me to find strength to believe in myself through the darkest nights to manifest this book.

And dearest to my heart, I thank God Almighty for his mercy, continued grace, and constant compassion.

Thank you and I love you all.

A special rest in peace blessing to my son, Willie.

Your smile will always be in my heart.

Introduction

I'm writing this book to share my knowledge learned though hard experiences. I don't want my girls, or any woman, to fall prey to players like me and other guys I knew. My wish for my daughters is for them to have happiness, strength in who they are and know that they are worthy of the best relationship possible.

As a man, I am sorry for my past immaturity. It took me a while to realize the long-term and negative effects of my manipulations. I share my experiences now to help women recognize the signs and put a stop to it.

Imagine the words of advice in this book coming from a brother, uncle, or father. You'll notice I use the term "baby girl," because even though each of my babies grows up to be a teen, then a young woman, then a woman, they will always be my baby girl.

I know that God has used me to help other people move forward because he has given me a multitude of help for my life through my loved ones.

If you'd like to share your thoughts or questions with me as you read this book, please contact me by email at w.mitch50@gmail.com

Thank you,
Willie (aka Marzell)

Table of Contents

You Are the Prize, Not Him 1

No One is Perfect, Remember That 5

Never Give Too Much All At Once 9

Why Do Boys Lie? 13

Why do boys cheat? 17

At What Age Are Boys Serious? 21

Should boys respect their mothers? 25

Lose Your Mind, Lose Control 29

Stand for You Or Fall for Him 33

If all else fails, move on! 37

About the Author 41

You Are the Prize, Not Him

"Back then I confused passions and orgasms with love. It took me years to realize the two weren't synonymous." ~Terry McMillan, Getting to Happy

I remember once, I had this "yep" girl that I dated. I used to ask her, "Aren't I the man?" "Yep, you sure are," she kept replying. I was arrogant as hell. I couldn't wait for my strings to form a mustache on my lips and hair on my chest. I knew that would make her want me even more. "Yep, you got that right," she said.

I was a known basketball player and she was the captain of her cheerleading squad. She had the whole package when it came to being a cheerleader. She was smart, funny, cute face, and very talented. My athletic talent seemed like it was the best in the world to her. Even though I was dumber than a box of rocks, she would still put me on a pedestal. When we walked around in school holding hands, people would come up to me, male and female, talking to me and not showing her any respect. I would just go along with their conversation not putting them in their place to show my girlfriend respect. See, baby girl, don't let his arrogant, masculine side fool you. I tell you this for your protection in the long run. Don't get caught up in the passion of the moment and allow him to just walk around with you on his arm as the prize while excluding you from the conversation. He is supposed to protect the prize, which is you.

You, you are the prize. A magical, beautiful prize that boys go after for a time. But when young, they don't understand that you could be more than the prize of the moment but could be the prize for a lifetime. Your self-worth is more than just a prize on a boy's arm.

Boys should dive into the deepest sea, climb the highest mountain, and fly to the highest of skies in order to obtain the cost of you. Yes, let him shower you with gifts when he can, or will, but don't give in too easily because of those gifts. I heard a wise man once say, "the key to a woman's heart is an unexpected gift, at an unexpected time." Even though he did it once or maybe even twice, keep him doing it again and again. Don't settle for allowing him to have your heart because of some gifts.

Live each day for the day because there is a lot to be learned about you. Tomorrow is its own, even if today's joy goes into tomorrow's coming. Always expect more because you are worth more even if you have given him some of the fruit between your legs. Remember he isn't the best in your world, you are! You are always the center of your own world. Who you let into and who you keep in your world is up to you.

You're like fuel to a vehicle. Just as a vehicle can't run without fuel, he's not at his best movement without you making him better. So, keep him doing the unexpected if he wants to receive any expectation from you. Remember you are the missing link to a broken chain. He doesn't produce achievements to attract male friends, he does it to attract you! It's a competition with another male as he tries to become the better competitor by allowing his male ego to drive him. But when he's around you, he is as soft as doctor's cotton.

Why is it that when he's around you, he feels like someone cares? Well, because he knows that you bring out the best in him. The things you do place his mind back in a secure state like he had with his mother when he was younger. So, don't ask for more, demand more! Let your actions speak louder than your words. Compete with him, but don't let him win. Let him know that you're the "shit." When you challenge him, he will bow down to you. You need to start this early in the relationship. It gets hard to attempt this later in the relationship because he didn't have to take you as seriously.

Go into the relationship knowing that you're the stock which he's investing into, and the only time your value will drop is when he doesn't invest more time into you.

Be careful, though, don't force a relationship that doesn't feel right just because you want to make him perfect for you or you perfect for him. If you have to end a relationship that just isn't working, it can leave a longing, an empty space in your heart, take that to heart. What was missing or not right? Learn from it. Remember you are the gift to him from God, not the other way around!

Baby Girl, ask yourself: Have you ever tried to force a relationship with a boy? What was the result?

No One is Perfect, Remember That

"Follow your instincts. That's where true wisdom manifests itself." ~Oprah Winfrey

I must hit this point directly. Baby girl, no human being is perfect, not by a long shot. Everyone has flaws, everyone! We are all going to make mistakes. Some people just never learn from them or they don't care that they're making mistakes and possibly hurting other people. Learning to value yourself, knowing that you will make mistakes, is important so you'll have the desire to correct those mistakes, move on, and do better.

A boy has to be willing, in his own mind, to want to be a trustworthy person. He may not notice his mistakes even though he keeps making them and getting the same results, over and over again. He won't see that he's making those mistakes until he notices that he is getting the same result, but that may take some time. You don't have to stick around while he figures that out.

There is an old saying that goes, "sometimes the person you're with could be setting you up for who you're supposed to be with." Yes, I know that the two of you might have this "great investment" of love, built up as high as the sky, where you forgive him again and again. The more you allow him to do things that need forgiveness, the more he will flip the whole problem onto you. Then you're going to feel the need to change your ways to make the relationship better. This is total manipulation! You have just been caught in the web of a slime ball! Guess what? He just ran game on you. If he can do that to you now, what more do you think he'll bring on the journey of your relationship?

Yes, we have flaws, but it's still our own good judgement call to know right from wrong. Pain doesn't feel good, right? So, quit taking it when you have a choice not to! If you haven't felt pain well, keep living, you will. It's part of life. Pain helps us create the desire to learn from and correct our mistakes and to feel better.

By accepting his manipulation, you are also giving him approval, approval to keep making those same mistakes. Through his arguments, he is showing you that he's not acknowledging his faults, not accepting his responsibilities. He is messing up, but he will put you into a mindset where you are trying to guess what you have done wrong for the relationship to be at this point. But know this, if something seems wrong, it probably is and it's not you!

Baby girl, statistics say girls are smarter through their early years and as they come of age. What makes you not so smart as you get older? Boys today are the same from an early age, because they keep searching in life for something; on the other hand, you are just trying to keep what you have in life.

Of course, you are the beautiful prize, but not every boy is the right match for you. And you are not always the right prize for every boy, no matter how much you think you want to be in the moment, no matter how much his manipulation has you second guessing yourself.

I came across some knowledge years ago that said, "girls are more prone to emotions while boys are more prone to vision." You see he does all the seeking while you are doing all the holding on. You are spending so much energy holding it together that you get to the point where you don't love yourself.

Remember when you were playing with your dolls and dollhouse and he was playing in the sandbox? Baby girl, while you were playing with your dolls, you were setting up a picture in your mind of how you wanted your house to be later in life. Meanwhile, he was building a sandcastle out of sand just so he could kick it all down when he was finished. He was putting a lie in his head that the whole thing was a waste of time. By himself, he doesn't know how to be constructive, but he is great at being destructive.

So, baby girl, I'm not saying that there isn't any good in any boy, just that you are going to have to find the right one and conform him into your world instead of allowing him to conform you completely to his world. And just because he's not perfect for you, doesn't mean he won't someday be perfect for someone else. Same goes for you – you might not be the perfect fit for a particular boy, but you will be the most amazing gift ever for the right boy and you'll know because it'll feel better than you could have imagined while playing with your dollhouse.

Baby Girl, ask yourself: How do you imagine your almost perfect relationship?

Never Give Too Much All At Once

"There is nothing in nature like it. Not in robins or bison or in the banging tails of your hunting dogs and not in blossoms or suckling foal. Love is divine only and difficult always. If you think it is easy you are a fool. If you think it is natural you are blind. It is a learned application without reason or motive except that it is God." ~Toni Morrison, Paradise

Early in high school, one of the best moments I recall was when I met a pretty girl in the first semester. We exchanged numbers and then we began to get to know each other's likes and dislikes. We shared some good laughs over silly things. She liked it when I sang to her, even though I didn't know how, because she loved R&B music. I desired to be her "Mr. Right." I tried to manifest myself into everything she could ever hope a guy could be because I always knew the reward for the both of us would be great afterwards. I knew that if I could become her Mr. Right, it would be much easier for me to maintain her approval.

To get what I wanted, I had her lying to her parents that she was going out to the movies with her girlfriends, and we would meet up for the movies ourselves. I'd manipulate her into smoking marijuana so that it relaxed her while we had sex. At home, she even started going to sleep early just so I could sneak over and climb through her window to lay with her.

Well after a while, the relationship started to get boring, repetitious. I was no longer interested in the usual. There was nothing left for me to chase after in order to receive, because I was getting physical pleasure from her every time we saw each other. So, we broke up on bad terms which ended up causing more pain to her than to me. I rebounded quickly with another girl and started all over with the same lame game I had used before.

This is an example of giving too much all at once or too soon without awareness of what was really going on in my quest for the prize that my young self was after. You should keep yourself a mystery or like a closed book that hasn't been read yet. There are a lot of things a boy needs to find out on his own about you; things a boy needs to learn become a man. For example, if you like chocolate, let him know and tell him what kind you like. Then you should leave it up to him to remember when it comes time to buying it for you. That starts to develop trust and you'll see if he's been paying attention. Tell him about your favorite colors, then weeks later ask him what your favorite colors are. Maybe take him shopping with you at the mall one day. Show him something you like, or don't like, whether it be long, short, cotton, nylon, silk, or whatever. Then weeks, months, or even a year later ask him to go out and buy you something really nice. Don't give him any ideas, just send him out on a mission. Then you will be able to see if he's been paying attention to your likes and dislikes.

Baby girl, you have to grade these boys like a report card! Just like with a report card, if you keep failing a certain class, your G.P.A. drops. If his G.P.A. keeps dropping, that's helpful information for you to use towards making a decision as to whether he is an asset or a liability in your life. You decide. I'm not telling you to not share with him things you like or don't like, but I'm saying don't tell him everything about you in a week, a month, or even a few days. Keep him chasing you like you're in the cartoon, "Tom & Jerry." Even though a girl is made for a boy, a boy gets empowerment from girls. See how much power is within you?

Boys don't dress to impress other boys. They are doing it for themselves and the attraction of you. Show him your words line up with your actions and expect the same from him. Boys are hunters, baby girl, and they are going to grow up to be full-grown men hunters. He will keep hunting till he has what he wants, but if he doesn't have it, he will keep hunting for it. So, baby girl, you need to be a hunter in a sense as well and keep grading him. Don't allow yourself to be preyed upon by the wrong guy who scored a low G.P.A. with you.

When you've been in a relationship a while, it'll get easier. He will be listening because he's practiced and you've required him to be paying attention and not just constantly hunting. He will get better at it. When you're committed to each other, you belong to each other in healthy ways, not abusive or possessive, but in mutually healthy ways.

Baby Girl, ask yourself: What are your relationship commandments or boundaries?

Why Do Boys Lie?

"If you don't like something, change it. If you can't change it, change your attitude." ~Maya Angelou

I remember my mother asking me, when I was a child, if I had "a dirty Pamper" after I had stood still and grunted for ten seconds. "Nope," I replied. "Come here," she said. When she could smell I had, she popped me right on my hand for lying to her. Years passed by and one day my teacher in elementary school called home to my mother and told her about my foolishness in class. I told my mother that it was caused by a boy mentioning something bad about her. Well, unknown to me, one day she was in the back of my classroom observing me being a damn fool. Class clown, I was. My mother came from behind and popped me upside my head. Oh man, I was embarrassed! The whole class laughed at what happened, but at the same time they feared adults.

So, the reason boys lie baby girl, is because they have been doing it from the very beginning. They were born into it. For him to slow down, he needs a transitional change in his life.

It's not guaranteed, but it's for him to experience. You can't give that to him, he must experience it for himself. Lying is like a virus, once it gets inside of you it spreads like wildfire. So, once started, it's hard to stop. It is something you have to deal with but dealing with how much is totally your call. He is likely going to lie about something to you. You're going to just have to weigh him out and see if he matches up with your beliefs.

Are all lies bad? If it causes any stress or pain to you what do you think? This is the question you should be asking yourself, does pain feel good? Baby girl, you have the right to make all judgements for yourself.

Don't let the lustful eye fool you from the truth. Just because he looks good, smells good, and kisses good, doesn't make him good. He could be a sheep in wolf's clothing. You need to be up front with your demands on the relationship. Tell him, "do not lie to me in this relationship." Let this be your first and most important commandment and everything else will come into the light behind this. Baby girl, you are the emotions of God and that's why your love is so strong. Even God wants you to be conscious of your awareness.

Stop putting so much into the relationship all at once. Take time to get to know one another. Don't go backwards in the process of getting to know one another. You know, like sex first then you tell him your name afterwards. The way you meet in the beginning affects how your relationship turns out in the end. The beginning is the root of your relationship, it speaks volumes.

Have you ever seen the "Maury" show? Lying boyfriends tell their girlfriends about such and such, and it's nothing but lies. Events like that could occur right at your own front door. So, what I'm telling you, baby girl, is to weigh out what is healthy and what is stressful to you. Be aware of what is happening around you and grade him on any lies. Watch that G.P.A. Were they little lies to avoid hurting your feelings or big ones that impact your relationship? You make the rules for your life and what you'll accept in your relationship.

Baby Girl, ask yourself: What lies have you been told or told yourself in a relationship?

Why do boys cheat?

"If she's amazing, she won't be easy. If she's easy, she won't be amazing. If she's worth it, you won't give up. If you give up, you're not worthy...Truth is, everybody is going to hurt you; you just gotta find the ones worth suffering for." ~Bob Marley

Baby girl, boys cheat on girls for many reasons, but there is one reason why they keep doing it. It's because you keep allowing it! Yeah, I know, you don't allow him to. I'm not trying to push his behavior back onto you. Remember when I mentioned earlier about the mystery you have to maintain about yourself? If he hasn't obtained all of you, he will keep coming after you until he has.

Baby girl, there are girls out there who are slime balls for all kinds of reason. Some girls will collect enough information from you so that they can form an idea in their mind of what it might be like to be with your man. Is that dirty or what?! So, if you have given your boy all of you too fast, one of those girls might just be able to steal him away.

After he has searched out all the mysteries about you, he has nothing else to seek after. You have to stay on a chase in a sense, like a cat after a mouse always on a run when they see each other, knowing that mouse might taste good to that cat if he were to catch him. Use absences as a sign of "When will I see you again?" from him. Stay seemingly too busy to be at his beck and call is what I'm saying.

Never let him have complete control of the relationship during the beginning or the end of the day. Use demands from time to time so that he doesn't see any weak submissiveness in you. You're gonna let him know you're headstrong by doing this. Boys really do like a challenging woman whether they admit it or not.

Keep your beauty regimes up, whatever they are. You're the next best thing to God. A woman that cares for her maintenance speaks a lot to him. It makes him want to know you more. Experience yourself with good perfumes, facial gloss that keeps you glowing, or whatever makes you feel good. When you feel good about yourself in that way, your confidence shows.

Those risks that are taken by him when he talks to another woman, and you have the evidence that he has, let it be known that you're not having it. If you feel in your mind that he's worth dealing with, put him in the dog pound outside. Make it tough for him to get in touch with you, make it seem like you're not interested anymore unless you really aren't. Let him know by your actions. You have to show him that you don't play games, that you say that you mean and you mean what you say.

Do you remember Beyoncé's song, "If I was boy?" Well, you need to do unto him as he would do unto you. Show him that you're not one that is going to sit around waiting for him all day long. If you call him and don't receive an answer, yet he expects you to answer every time he calls, don't accept that. If you challenge him face to face, he will change his action in an instant. I'm not saying that everything about him will change in an instant, but something will change, believe that.

If he sees you out with a smile on your face, that will bother him, only because he sees you out with others smiling. If you could capture the expression on his face, you would laugh even harder at the moment. Boys are greedy, baby girl, when they see you having fun without them, they get really jealous.

So, don't you sit there and accept a boy cheating on you. Get up, get out, and live life!

Remember this so that you will know offhand that every boy, at some point, is going to cheat you out of the full potential he has towards you. It's up to you to decide how much you are going to accept and how much you are going to give; otherwise, he will start sounding like a broken record in your ear asking you for forgiveness over and over again. Does this forbid you from being with a boy? No, not at all. God made us to be in unison with each other regardless of all the mess-ups we have with one another. Through those mess-ups, we are supposed to learn, grow, and pass on the knowledge.

So, baby girl what you need to do is be up front with him and tell him that what he won't do in the relationship someone else will. Distance yourself away from him from time to time and give each other space. Then when you are back together with him make it seem like you two were on deployment and there's an excitement to see each other.

Baby Girl, ask yourself: How do you handle jealousy?

At What Age Are Boys Serious?

"The times may have changed, but the people are still the same. We're still looking for love, and that will always be our struggle as human beings." ~Halle Berry

Boys are serious at what they know at that moment involving relationships with you. If they knew better, they would do better, but he's acting out from examples he learned and that has affected his judgement. It's gonna take a process to show him better.

Listen, boys mature differently than girls. From their teens to their 20s, it's like they're on a trampoline bouncing around, never ending on the same landing. Life is like that trampoline to him. He's here, there, everywhere, trying to figure out who and what he is. Then, from his 20s-30s, he's looking to have a successful career where money is coming in. And in his 30s-40s, he wants to have a serious relationship, someone he can love and be in love with, a house, a child or two, and the white picket fence. In his 50s, maybe it didn't work out exactly or maybe he messed all the above up. He might just settle with whomever wants him and that could be a sad life for the two of them.

Your first relationship is an experience that teaches you how to have a relationship. Yes, some people's first relationship becomes a marriage to their life mate, but many times there are great consequences behind it. This happens because you don't have enough experience to know what your likes and dislikes are. When someone new comes around and gives you a new and different feeling inside of your head, it's like "wow" to you. It becomes foreign to everything that you were taught and it can make you want to explore what you never knew.

Baby girl, for you, finding the right guy is like experiencing used cars until you have saved up enough money to buy that new vehicle you want! But until then, you settle for good enough and it goes on until you get it right and are truly satisfied, that just depends on you. But remember, your life isn't over just because you're still in the used car phase, so don't feel like giving up. Keep going until you find him.

I mentioned earlier that boys need you more than you need them. You can look at him sometimes and tell if you really want to be bothered with him. On the other hand, he can look at you and act like a fool just to make you say something to him. Your knowledge and his acts are two opposite sides of attraction, but you are attracted to that which appeals to you. Don't let an unbalanced relationship spoil you and dictate that you make bad decisions for the rest of your life. Don't be like that fool. Baby girl, boys have a lot to do with your character development and you have a lot to do with his character development. In a sense, he characterizes your mindset as to what type of guy you are looking for.

Let's say that a boy asks you to try drugs, and you decide to give it a try. You like it and then that relationship doesn't last. Now, your future relationships could be tampered by your last experience in a drug-related relationship. The same can be done to him by you. These relationships are a learning experience for you both until you finally find the one that seems odd, new, and different from the ones that you have had in the past.

So, for him being serious comes out at what age? It would be when he is in his mid-30s to early 40s. That is when he really starts to take things seriously. The world seems like a big ol' trampoline to him in his earlier years. Now, the choice is yours to decide at what age you feel you will be able to trust him. That doesn't mean you should go out and look for a much older guy to have in your life. Of course, even that may be okay if you are truly attracted to older guys and it doesn't cause any problem with your family.

Just be aware that his seriousness level could be different than yours at different stages of your lives. When you're both young, don't expect him to automatically stop that trampoline jumping. It's still exciting to him, life is an adventure waiting to happen. If you can jump on the trampoline with him sometimes, it shows that you are trying to understand him.

You might be ready for the household you dreamed up as a little girl, but he's probably not going to be ready for that for a while. So live your life and make your best choices and if he really feels like the right guy, then try to mature with him rather than trying to force him to catch up with you.

Baby Girl, ask yourself: When do you think you'll be ready for a more serious relationship?

Should boys respect their mothers in order to respect me?

"Passion is energy. Feel the power that comes from focusing on what excites you." ~Oprah Winfrey

Respect towards his mother could be very helpful towards him understanding the value of you. It can help him in many ways, such as knowing how to approach you in a respectful manner, positioning himself to be a help to you rather than being more of a harm. So, yes, he should respect his mother or he won't have the proper ideas to be able to respect you. He would think of you as just another boy in the sandbox. Boys in the sandbox kick, knock each other over, yell, and play with each other extremely hard.

One of the hardest jobs for him is to understand you. His world will be centered around you. I read a great book that said, "you are the land and everything that is in the land has to harvest off of its caregiver, so whatever type of guy you are dealing with, you will harvest his seed to the world." You would love for him to have some sort of caring emotions in himself because an emotional boy will, in a sense, be able to confide with an emotional girl.

Every boy has a feminine side because of the genes he inherited from his mother. There are some that have more than others. The reason why his feminine side doesn't show much is because he's always around the male gender. When he comes around you, he becomes broken down like a common denominator, acting like a little child, holding onto your leg. This, of course, is something that he did around his mother when he was a child in order to gain a sense of security. If he can put up with a mother's love, then he definitely can put up with yours.

Find out how close he is with his mother. See where their relationship stands concerning respect. If his mother isn't in his life, find out why. If there is another female in his life that he respects like a mother, find out about her. Searching for these things will help you understand who and what you are dealing with. Instead of searching for a loving relationship when you know each other's compatibility, he could be searching for a mother. Then guess what? You will find yourself being his mother and that could make you very mad. Have you ever found yourself cleaning up his mess or wiping his mouth every time he eats or making him blow his nose when he doesn't realize he has to? Do you have to remind him to wash his face? Brush his teeth? Now that might sound like too much, but does that also sound like you?

So, yes, I believe having an inspiring woman in his life or having a woman he respected will help to groom his knowledge about your worth to his life. This is because the two of you becoming in unison brings out the best in each other. There is power in numbers. One has to be able to lift the other up when they fall. Both can't be negative or there will be no positive result. A man's values are different than a women's values when it comes to teaching respect. A man teaches a boy to fight for what he wants, and a woman teaches him to love what he has.

Baby Girl, ask yourself: What about girls – do you think your respect for your father, or other male figure, impacts your relationships with boys?

Lose Your Mind, Lose Control

"If everything was perfect, you would never learn and you would never grow." ~Beyonce Knowles

Now, when you let a boy have control over your mind, you will lose control over yourself. See, after he becomes "Mr. Prince" to you, within a week, month, or even a year, your thoughts will become his thoughts, and whatever he decides on, you will do the same.

I know one person that is great at controlling your mind, this man is a magician. He is so good at trickery that he can get you to believe that a skyscraper can disappear into thin air. He says that after so many years of building them that he can make them disappear in ten minutes. Please!

It is the same with you, baby girl. After so many years growing up in life, suddenly one day you started acting up outside of your normal character because of your relationship with a boy. Your future comes to a crossroad with his. Baby girl, the honest truth is that you need to give him space. Cluttering him every day, all day, having your life too dependent on his will soon have you both worn out and you will be wondering what went wrong.

Once again, do not go chasing after him, let him chase after you! Who is the prize here? You are like a matching Powerball ticket on a Friday night. Believe that! Get him interested in your future. Work it out together and support each other's goals so that if this doesn't work out for the both of you, you will still have your life.

Remember earlier when I mentioned that boys are hunters? Always keep giving him reasons to chase after you. Give in and give out in such a way that he is unable to figure you out immediately. This will serve to place a guard on your emotions for the unexpected that he will perform. It's going to happen, don't doubt that, but this will allow the fall to change from a terrifying experience to a learning one.

The longer that you date someone, the more you will learn to know yourself and how to interact in relationships. Experiences become great teachers in our own lives. This is something that no one else can teach you. You have to live out the story which God has already written for you. Allow some advice to come from others, baby girl.

We are the best creatures that God ever created on this earth; however, you are greater, because God created you to help the right boy that he has placed in your direction towards achievement. So, in other words, you are God's substitute teacher to mankind. See how much power you have inside yourself which is coming from a higher power. Wow! If you don't want your DNA, could you please give it to someone that will use it?

Baby girl, you need to know and believe your worth under this sun which we live. You're like the sun during its early morning rise, lifting up everything under it. Just as the sun causes flowers that appear dead to come alive, you bring life into a boy's eyes. You make him want to know what it feels like to become a man.

So, why should you lose your mind and body over a damn fool? Some person taught him to be a fool, so he uses those tools and learns to become a damn fool. Does that make sense? You are second in line under God, tied with the air which he created so that we could live. Know That!

Baby Girl, ask yourself: What is the gift of you in a relationship? Or what have you learned about yourself though past relationships?

Stand for You Or Fall for Him

"You can and should set your own limits and clearly articulate them. This takes courage, but it is also liberating and empowering, and often earns you new respect."
~Rosalind Brewer

I remember my relationship with this certain girl. What I thought was going to last forever suddenly came to short notice. I did things that were wrong, only because I knew that she would put up with them and because she would put up with me. One day, she said to me, "you keep disappearing on me and you're going to find someone taking your place." Sure enough, I did. When I later tried to prove to her that I was "Mr. Right," well, "Mr. Replacement" already had a higher G.P.A. than I did. Wow, I didn't even realize what a great thing I had until it was gone.

Baby girl, quit accepting deceitful lies from boys, especially the one where he says, "I won't do it again, I promise." Yeah, sure! It will be something different next time. Your word means everything, so tell him your commandments and never repeat them again unless it's to cut his butt loose. What has become old to him is still new to someone else. Believe that!

Don't let too many days, weeks, months go by where he is "having fun" with you. For instance, you send him out to get you some sort of treats or refreshments, but instead of buying things you like, he buys things he likes for you to have. Many little things like that can add up and become a very big thing. If you allow this, he will set in his brain that you wouldn't mind what he brings. That is a no-no! If the store doesn't have what you want, well, he should have his cell phone in his hand, calling you and asking you what else you might like. That goes a long way, believe me. It will get to the point where you would hear him saying to his friends, "Man, my girl doesn't play like that." He will do this because he is receptive to your choices.

Baby girl, surf the internet and look at all the great men in this world that have come and gone. Look at the people they have acknowledged as having great influences on their life and you are bound to find a woman's name mentioned. Stand for what you have, which is a power from a higher being, God almighty.

Don't approach a boy being gullible because he will feed off your vibe and have you for lunch, which means just another meal to be eaten. Don't let low esteem bring everything in you down, whether it's weight, looks, confidence, or even a lack of friends. Recreate you! What brings others around you to where they notice something different about you? You've got to become new and attractive.

Baby girl, always remember that there is someone for everyone living here on God's green earth. Love you so that love can radiate out from you to where others notice it. Seek out information to know more about you and your own ways. Find out your role here on earth, and I promise your confidence level will be sky-high and neither birds nor planes will be able to reach up to you.

Baby Girl, ask yourself: What is something that you've learned you can not accept in a relationship?

If all else fails, move on!

"There is nothing a woman can't do. Men might think they do things all by themselves but a woman is always there guiding or helping them." ~Marjorie Joyner

Loving yourself first is the most important start towards having a relationship outside of the one you are in. Do not be afraid of leaving him. If all the signs add up to where the both of you aren't balanced in the relationship, then let it go. Don't second guess yourself. If he really wants you, he will notice a good thing when it's gone. Then he would have to put in a double shift to obtain you again. If he truly cares, he won't mind having to do so. But in all honesty, don't lose your mind over that knuckle-headed boy. Use him as a learning tool. If you feel that you have to choose another route, well, do so, baby girl, it's your life.

I was told that there are three things that you learn in life, and you will die knowing them. I don't mean an immediate death, but whenever God says that your time has come. Those three things are observation, association, and education. Now, we tend to focus on one more than the others. But what I'm telling you, baby girl, is to focus on all three so that you have the knowledge you need to fight whatever is in your face. You can observe others who have gone through similar situations as you have. You can associate with an experienced survivor or you can educate yourself through self-help books.

One thing about relationships is that there is someone out there in this world for everyone. Don't be the young lady, "looking back," the one who's gotten older, has a child, loves her child but wishes it wasn't by this damn fool. You don't want to have to deal with this damn fool for the rest of your life while you and many others in your family don't like him. Baby girl, do you realize that your relationship with a damn fool can cause a division with some really supportive loved ones in your life? This is because they can spot a slimeball a mile away. This may be due to them having a similar chapter in their life or maybe they can just witness a damn fool's behavior. Don't just hear them, listen to them.

Think about this, maybe he isn't loving you but just lusting after you. I know you should know the difference between the two. If you don't, well, know that he should be sacrificing himself in making himself available to your needs, and the rewards will be balanced. If not, move on!

Baby Girl, ask yourself: Do you believe that you are strong enough to move on if you ever need to?

RIP

Pillars Of My Strength

About the Author

Marzell Mitchell, aka Willie, enjoys sharing his often hard-learned wisdom about relationships and the games boys will often play in those relationships. As a teen and young man he didn't appreciate nor respect women the way he does today.

Today, he recognizes and wants every woman at any age, to know their worth and demand respect. Women should know their value of what they really mean to men – the value that they don't always show.

He hopes that with this advice, women can decide what is acceptable and unacceptable in their relationships and that they can build strength in themselves to know they deserve better.

Willie enjoys speaking to groups, sharing on podcasts and radio shows. You can get in touch with him by email at w.mitch50@gmail.com

Made in the USA
Monee, IL
15 April 2021